A HISTORY OF
AMERICAN ART
PORCELAIN

A HISTORY OF
AMERICAN ART
PORCELAIN

By MARVIN D. SCHWARTZ
and RICHARD WOLFE

RENAISSANCE EDITIONS, NEW YORK

Library of Congress catalog card number 66-30197
Copyright © 1967 by Renaissance Editions, Inc., New York City
No part of this book may be reproduced in any form
without permission in writing from the publisher.
Manufactured in the United States of America
Composition by Frost Bros., Inc., New York City
Printed by Reehl Litho., Inc., New York City
Bound by American Book-Stratford Press, New York City
Designed by Vincent Ceglia, Trenton, New Jersey

Second Printing, October 1967

TABLE OF CONTENTS

FOREWORD

During the past decade a great many books have been published about the Arts of the United States, but this compact volume is the first to be devoted exclusively to the subject of American porcelain.

Mr. Schwartz, who is a distinguished authority in the field of American decorative arts, is eminently qualified to treat this specialized subject. Mr. Wolfe's many years of association with the publishing of books on the arts makes him a most valuable co-author. Their concise and highly readable survey of the development of the manufacture of porcelain in the United States from the middle of the 18th century to the present, is a significant contribution to the bibliography of American art.

The book has served as the basis for a historical exhibition of American porcelain which will circulate to several dozen American and European museums during the next three years.

STUART P. FELD,

Associate Curator of American Paintings and Sculpture, The Metropolitan Museum of Art

A HISTORY OF
AMERICAN ART
PORCELAIN

CHAPTER I
The Heritage of Porcelain

The art of making porcelain began and was developed more than a thousand years ago in China. Throughout the centuries, almost everywhere in the world, artisans have struggled to obtain the secrets of porcelain making, and connoisseurs have sought fine porcelain as a mysterious and magnificent treasure. Its attraction remains intense in our time. In 1966, a prized Louis XV clock brought the highest price ever paid for a single piece of porcelain—$82,320.

When Marco Polo first saw porcelain in the Orient, he thought it looked like *porcellana,* or "cowrie shell," which he had admired at home in Italy. Thus the name porcelain is derived from the Italian word and credited to the explorer. The fascination with Chinese porcelain led to the development of a ware in which Chinese designs were copied, but no effort was made to reproduce the porcelain body. Actually, porcelain is a form of ceramics. It is stronger than other ceramic bodies, yet thin enough to be translucent because it is made of special clays that have been fired at very high temperatures.

Porcelain making developed in China during the Tang Dynasty (A. D. 618-907) and the beginning of the Sung Dynasty (960-1279). Sources in Western literature reveal that Oriental porcelain was known to Europeans as early as the 12th century. However, it was not until the period of the Ming Dynasty (1368-1644) that Europeans became familiar with these wares and began to imitate them.

Europe was escaping darkness: Johann Gutenberg revolutionized the world by inventing movable type, and Columbus expanded the world by discovering America. Europeans were drawn to the mysterious art of the Orient. For them the great secret of porcelain lay in the nature of the ingredients. It was difficult to discern that there were three closely related factors: the two basic ingredients (kaolin and feldspar) and the temperature of the kiln. From the start, it was possible to achieve the appearance of porcelain, yet not its strength. Frequently, glass was substituted for the feldspar. This produced a glass and clay variation called "soft paste," which may have persisted because it required less heat than "hard" or true porcelain. Soft paste continued to be made in many places even after the secret of hard porcelain had been discovered.

The first European porcelain was made during the 15th century. Although the first factory did not exist for long, the experiment was repeated several times in the next century. During this period, an early, but unsuccessful attempt in the Western history of trying to gain the secret of porcelain was the appearance of the famed Medici pieces in Florence. These blue and white wares reflect Chinese and Near-Eastern influences; some pieces have a grayness of body that relates them to Persian wares. The next important attempts to produce porcelain in Europe occurred in France, at Rouen in the 1670's, and at St. Cloud, from 1677 until as late as 1764. But once again these wares used soft paste.

The search for the true porcelain was an activity that absorbed the time and talents of many artisans, and the 18th century is studded with their names. The honor of making the first true porcelain in Europe goes to an alchemist named Johann Friedrich Böttger, who worked in the Meissen factory near Dresden. Böttger's triumph occurred in 1713. Thereafter, other factories, hiring workmen from Meissen, were able to learn the secret of the newly perfected hard porcelain. Even so, the process spread slowly and some soft paste continued to be made.

True porcelain and even soft-paste porcelain were expensive enough to inspire a continued interest in other less costly wares that offered some of the qualities of porcelain. Böttger himself produced a quantity of fine stoneware. It was more brittle than porcelain, but it was strong and useful. In England, John Dwight made such stoneware, calling it porcelain, as early as 1671. Some fifty years later, when this ware was covered with a salt glaze that made it as white as true porcelain, it became popular as a relatively inexpensive imitation.

The ceramic industry grew steadily in the 1700's. At about the same time that the salt glaze was introduced, high-fire earthenwares with a white body were developed. These were first glazed in one of several polychrome surfaces, such as simulated marble or tortoise shell. The result was called "Whieldon ware" after Thomas Whieldon, one of the more prominent Staffordshire potters of the 18th century.

Josiah Wedgwood, a famous name in ceramics, contributed to the improvement of earthenware during this era by perfecting a cream-colored glaze. This was called creamware, and later, queen's ware (honoring his patron, Queen Charlotte). In the 19th century, the mass-produced Staffordshire creamwares were gradually replaced by stoneware or graniteware, a hard, higher-fired ceramic body closer to porcelain.

Actually, all of these fine earthenwares, which we admire, were still essentially the poor man's porcelain. They were indeed significant on the English and American scenes. England's development in porcelain got under way rather late. The earliest piece of English porcelain is dated 1745. On the Continent, similar advancements were taking place in the famous factories of Meissen and Sèvres. But it was not until the late 17th century that this treasured heritage, spanning eleven hundred years, was brought to America.

CHAPTER II
The Beginning of Porcelain Manufacture
in America: 18th Century

The newly emerging American arts—both fine and decorative—were typically plain and functional. They have been called medieval in that the structural elements are basic design factors with decorative motifs of the late Renaissance often applied as ornament. A fine example of the American furniture of the period is the oak blanket chest manufactured in New England which is decorated with flat carvings of floral motifs and arches. Brown-glazed red earthenwares were the ceramics most widely used.

Toward the end of the 17th century, the Baroque style, characterized by much ornamentation and curved rather than straight lines, became fashionable. In its American version it was called the William and Mary style, but it had the ingredients of fashions encountered during the reigns of Charles II, his immediate successsors, and Louis XIV. The Baroque is a dramatic style, and in its best architecture there are surprising changes in pace and scale. One manifestation of this spirit in the decorative arts was the use of "classical" objects, along with Oriental porcelain. The "classical" objects were well-proportioned and symmetrical with subtle refinements based on Greco-Roman designs.

In America, "delftware" was occasionally referred to as porcelain or "china," although it is much thicker than porcelain in body. Evidence that delftware was made as early as 1685 in the vicinity of Burlington, New Jersey, is available in the records of a legal dispute involving a man who managed a delftware pottery. An account of the pottery by Dr. Daniel Cox, one of the proprietors of the Colony of West New Jersey, has been uncovered at the Bodleian Library at Oxford University. Writing in 1689, Dr. Cox reported: "I have erected a pottery at Burlington for white and Chiney ware, a great quantity to ye value of 1200 li [English pounds] have been already made and vended in ye County, neighbor colonies and ye Islands of Barbados and Jamaica. . ." The ware was probably very similar to English delftware. A surviving fragment, a tile attributed to the Burlington factory, is covered with a white glaze that might well be the same sort of tin oxide used on delft.

The most significant factor in the evidence of this pottery is that there should have been an effort so early in American history to set up a workshop that brought together a team of skilled workmen and an elaborate kiln. In spite of the difficulties inherent in establishing a pottery in Colonial America, sufficient incentive doubtless was provided by the high cost of importing wares and potters. Up to now, there has been no opportunity to excavate the site of the Cox pottery to determine the range of the wares produced there, or to press the search locally and in the Caribbean.

About 1725 there was a change of style that involved a basic change in concept. The monumental aspects of the Baroque were replaced by one having an architectural intimacy. The American designer simplified the ornamental motifs, which were mainly from the same repertory of design in the new style, the Rococo, as the old. The Rococo was the style of art and architecture developed in France from the Baroque and characterized primarily by elaborate ornamentation imitating foliage, rockwork, shellwork, scrolls, etc., often done with much delicacy and refinement. It was popular especially in the first half of the 18th century. During this important period in the development of porcelain, the Classical motifs tended to be handled asymmetrically or whimsically by the Rococo designer. Naturalistic, Oriental and Gothic details were sometimes introduced to reduce the emphasis of the Classical impact. Porcelain is a perfect medium for small sculpture and therefore was particularly appropriate for the Rococo.

After the first real porcelain was made at Meissen in Saxony in 1713, there were a succession of efforts to make porcelain all over Europe. Many of these were subsidized by local governments and met with a measure of success in the ensuing decades. In England, where no official assistance was forthcoming, the quest for real porcelain was slower in achieving success. Meanwhile America showed the first stirrings of the art. The earliest piece of dated English porcelain, the Chelsea jug of 1745, was made a few years after a patent application to establish a monopoly in the production of porcelain was submitted by the American potter, Andrew Duché.

Duché, the son of a Huguenot potter, was born in Philadelphia and had been working in Savannah, Georgia, when he claimed to be ". . . the first man in Europe, Africa or America that ever found the true material and manner of making porcelain or China ware." In a report of December 29, 1739, the Governor of Georgia wrote:

> "Andrew Duché is the Potter at Savannah who goes on very well there is one of the most industrious in the Town and had made several Experiments which seem to look like the making of China."

The success of the experiments is suggested in a report of 1741, when William Stephens, Secretary of the Colony, described Duché's ware as translucent and said that Duché planned to go to England and show his work to the trustees of the Colony.

European and English potters working in the Rococo style, used designs adapted from silver and figures. Naturalistic or rustic qualities were important and Oriental models were also used. Duché was probably better acquainted with Oriental than European porcelains.

As a knowledgeable potter, he had discovered the proper clays for porcelain after reading accounts of porcelain manufacture by du Halde that were published in the 18th century from observations made in the Orient. One example attributed to him is a bowl that appears to be an experimental piece in blue and white. Both Oriental and Western motifs appear on it.

The next record of an effort to make porcelain is not encountered until almost thirty years later. In 1766, an American Society for the Encouragement of Arts and Manufactures made an award to Samuel Bowen "for his useful observations in china and industrious application of them in Georgia." Arthur Clement, one of the finest students of the history of American ceramics, questions interpreting the award as evidence that Bowen made porcelain and rather prefers to assume that he was in some way involved in the shipping of porcelain clay to England. Various references to the fine quality of American clay were made by the English potters from the 1740's to the 1760's when Josiah Wedgwood was experimenting with "Cherokee clay," a fine clay found in Georgia and related to kaolin. Duché had promoted its use in the 1740's.

Josiah Wedgwood's name is associated with documenting another figure in the history of American porcelain. In 1765, Wedgwood expressed concern that a pottery was being set up in South Carolina because, he wrote, ". . . they have every material there, equal, if not superior to our own for carrying on that manufacture." Later, his concern about this competitor was allayed when he heard who would head the enterprise; he dismissed the man as ". . . one of our insolvent master potters." Wedgewood's references are thought to apply to John Bartlam, who advertised in the *South Carolina Gazette* in 1770 and 1771.

In the issue of October 4, 1770, Bartlam announced:

"A China Manufactory and Pottery is soon to be opened in this town, on the lot [of the] late Mr. Hougetts, by Messrs Bartlam & Company, the proper hands, etc. for carrying it having lately arrived from England. . ."

Several months later, on January 31, 1771, the progress of the enterprise was reported:

"John Bartlam, Having opened his Pottery and China-Manufactory in Old Church Street, Will be much obliged to Gentlemen in the Country, or others, who will be so kind to send him samples of any Kinds of fine Clay upon their Plantations . . . He already makes Queen's Ware equal to any imported. . ."

No further mention of Bartlam's enterprise has been uncovered nor is there any porcelain or creamware identified as the work of Bartlam. Also, in the 1760's, in Germantown,

PLATE 2. *Sauce boat. Made by Bonnin & Morris, Philadelphia, circa 1771-1772. Mark: Outside base a small "p" in pale blue under the glaze. Height: 4". Length: 7⅜". Courtesy of The Brooklyn Museum.*

PLATE 3. *Fruit basket. Made by Bonnin & Morris in the Southwark Section of Philadelphia, circa 1770. This is one of the earliest securely documented pieces of American porcelain. Height: 3". Courtesy of the Philadelphia Museum of Art.*

CHAPTER III

The Empire Style
in American Porcelain: 1810-1850

The American Revolution coincided with the introduction of Neoclassicism. This new style, a reaction against the excesses of Rococo, was characterized by the revival of ancient Greco-Roman design. It can be traced back to the 1740's when the intellectual expatriates residing in Rome began to attempt historical accuracy in recording Roman history and mythology. They were the first of an extensive group of artists to emphasize the historical context of events, and their studies influenced architects and designers whose research into vocabularies of ornament became more intense.

Although this first group of artists was unusually mediocre, the next generation included great talents from various parts of Europe. The British architect, Robert Adam, one of the foremost exponents of the new style, discovered it in the 1750's. He selected Greco-Roman motifs that could be rendered in the delicate linear style that he preferred. Robert Adam is thought to have influenced the French and to have anticipated the architects and designers of the French court of Louis XVI in introducing the linear ornament of Neoclassicism.

In ceramics, the prime figure of this period was Josiah Wedgwood, who produced fine stoneware bodies, basalt and jasper ware for designs in the Neoclassical spirit. Oriental designs continued to be prominent in the porcelain field, but straight-sided cups decorated with delicate linear ornament were introduced.

On the American scene there seems to be no porcelain surviving from the period between the Revolution and the beginning of the 19th century, when the first phase of the Neoclassical style flourished. Utilitarian stonewares—big storage jugs and the like—were produced in quantity, but the only evidence of porcelain making are the documents recording the foundation of the Boston Porcelain and Glass Company. This factory operated for about a year, and if it produced anything it would have been wares in the Neoclassical pattern.

The lack of surviving work from potteries active in the period is particularly unfortunate because there are records showing that a number of organizations awarded prizes for wares. In about 1787, the Pennsylvania Society for the Encouragement of Manufacturers awarded a gold plate for the "best specimen of Pennsylvania-made earthenware approaching the nearest in quality to the Delft, white stone, or queen's ware. . ." These documents provide the only proof of the existence of potteries capable of producing these fine earthenwares.

Philadelphia and Trenton were the centers of pottery production noted for quality.

There are many references in the advertisements of potters working elsewhere who claimed their work to be as fine as that done in these centers. Records of creamware made in Philadelphia include the work of Alexander Trotter, who in 1818 exhibited examples from his Columbian Pottery, a "queen's ware manufactory," at Peale's Museum. A short time later, David G. Seixas was listed in the Philadelphia Directory as the manufacturer of creamware, "similar to Liverpool."

By the time porcelain manufacturing was flourishing in America, Neoclassicism had passed into a second phase called the Empire style. This European style which embodies Classical and Egyptian motifs, became fashionable in 1804 when Napoleon I became Emperor of France. Most notably, this style involved a change in proportion and an attempt to adhere more closely to the Greco-Roman models. In the first phase of Neoclassicism, the ornament had been light in scale and forms in the main bore no relation to the ancient models that served as inspiration. The fascination for the ancient increased, and as designers became more aware of the arts of Greece and Rome, there was a greater effort to follow the Classical models more closely.

Apart from the interest in Classical art, a philosophical connection was made. Democracy had its roots in Greece and the governments of Greece and Rome were studied by political theoreticians newly aware of history. Ironically, Napoleon's study of Rome seems to have given him the inspiration to move from being a Consul in the Roman sense to being crowned Emperor. He also was such an avid enthusiast of Roman design that Neoclassicism appealed to him and his surroundings were decorated in a version of the Roman style. This was of tremendous influence all over the Western world during the early 19th century.

In America, the shift from the early to the later Neoclassicism, or Empire style, is most easily seen in a comparison between two popular chair designs. The shield-back chair, commonly called the Hepplewhite chair, is the earlier type. It is a purely 18th-century invention using details such as the shield and delicately carved floral ornament which are derived from ancient sources. The later approach is evident in the typical Duncan Phyfe chair, which is based on an ancient Greek model.

The first example of American porcelain in the Empire style is a vase that was made in a factory owned by a New York physician, Dr. Henry Mead. There is some confusion about the dating and origin of the one example attributed to him—a handsome white vase in a simple Classical shape with caryatid handles (Plate 5, page 24). It turned up in the collections of the Franklin Institute with a paper label attached stating that it was completed in 1816. Norman Gregor-Wilcox discovered that in J. Leander Bishop's *History of American Manufacturers* the Mead factory is said to have been started in 1819 in New York, while Mead's obituary has him as "a man of genius and enterprise being the first who ever manufactured porcelain or china in this country which he commenced at Jersey City." One date is obviously incorrect, but an explanation lies in the fact that many New York ceramic shops had their wares made in New Jersey, where local clay deposits made manufacturing easier.

The Mead vase is an example of soft-paste porcelain that is very close in spirit to French examples of the time. That Mead continued the undertaking for a few years is suggested by a document published by Arthur Clement. In a petition dated December 11, 1820, he addresses a request to the New York Common Council for the appointment of a committee "To confer with him on the practicability of employing the paupers in the Alms House and criminals in the Penitentiary in the manufacture of porcelain." Although the size of his enterprise is not known, it probably continued for several years, and very likely there are surviving pieces which have been considered work of the Paris shops that flourished in the period. Paris had many porcelain shops in the early 19th century. Their work ranged in quality from great to gruesome. A connoisseur at a loss with a piece of porcelain of the period logically called it "Paris."

Also unidentified are the products by Abraham Miller of Philadelphia, which earned him an award in 1824 from the Franklin Institute, where he exhibited a "specimen of porcelain and white ware" along with red and black glazed tea and coffee pots and a luster pitcher. Miller was well known for the more ordinary wares that he manufactured. The Jersey Porcelain and Earthenware Company, incorporated in 1825, was awarded a silver medal in 1826 for exhibiting "the best China from American materials." Fragments of bisque and glazed wares have been found on the site of the factory. A piece of glazed porcelain which was in the Trumbull-Prime Collection—until the collection was lost—typified porcelain in the Empire style: a bold, heavy shape with a plain gold band as decoration.

The most productive and significant porcelain manufacture in the Empire style was begun by William Ellis Tucker in 1826 (Plate 4, page 23). The son of a Philadelphia schoolteacher and china merchant, Tucker had tried his hand at decorating European porcelain "blanks" before embarking on his more ambitious project of manufacturing porcelain. After working first with a small kiln, the Tuckers (the father, Benjamin, and

William) leased a building known as the Old Waterworks at what is today Twenty-third and Chestnut in Philadelphia. They also purchased acreage in Chester County, Pennsylvania, and Middlesex County, New Jersey, to gain access to the proper clays.

In the course of the Tucker undertaking there were several partners involved. The earliest partner, John Bird, never seems to have taken part in the business. Thomas Hulme, the next associate, bought his share in 1828, and for less than a year was sufficiently active so that wares marked Tucker and Hulme survive. A third partner, Alexander Hemphill, joined Tucker in 1831. This new partnership resulted in an expansion. After the death of William in 1832, the enterprise was continued by Alexander's father, Judge Joseph Hemphill, with William's brother, Thomas, as manager. The factory was closed in 1838 after twelve years of fine production (Plate 7, page 26).

Tucker porcelain is a beautiful ware that includes a great variety of forms. It won its first award in 1827 from the Franklin Institute "for the best porcelain made in Pennsylvania, either plain or gilt," and the judges commented that "the body of this ware appeared to be strong, and sufficiently well fired, the glaze generally very good, the gilding executed in a neat and workmanlike manner. Some of the cups and other articles bear a fair comparison with those which were being imported."

The tea set by Tucker at The Brooklyn Museum, which is decorated simply in sepia scenes, may very well be an example of the early work. The pot, creamer and plates are in simple Grecian style while the cups curve in a design that would appear to be a simplification of an Oriental model. In Tucker ware, gilt decoration formed the borders of a number of pieces, and one popular form, the pitcher, was derived from ancient models with a reeded base reminiscent of the silver of the period. Painted decoration sometimes consisted of scenes and at other times was in the form of handsome floral motifs that were recorded in the Tucker pattern books preserved at the Philadelphia Museum.

Thomas Tucker's reminiscences and the accounts preserved with the factory records show the rich variety of their output. Decorative lamps, tea sets, dinner ware and handsome vases, jugs and pitchers were on the price list or were included as drawings in the pattern book.

Other manufacturers who worked in Philadelphia, producing a similar but probably a more limited range of wares were Smith, Fife & Co., and Kurlbaum & Schwartz (Plate 6, page 25 and Plate 8, page 26).

PLATE 4. *Bisque busts of children. These very rare pieces came down in the Tucker family. Made by the William Ellis Tucker Factory, Philadelphia, circa 1825-1838. Height: 7$\frac{1}{16}$". Courtesy of The Henry Ford Museum, Dearborn, Michigan.*

PLATE 5. *Vase. Produced by the factory of Dr. Henry Mead in New York, 1816. Height: 9½". Courtesy of the Philadelphia Museum of Art.*

PLATE 6. *Cake plate. Made by Kurlbaum & Schwartz, Philadelphia, circa 1853. Courtesy of the Philadelphia Museum of Art.*

PLATE 7. *Pitcher with painted scene. Made by Tucker & Hemphill, American China Manufactory, Philadelphia, circa 1830. Courtesy of the Philadelphia Museum of Art.*

PLATE 8. *Pitcher (one of a pair). Made by Smith & Fife Company, Philadelphia, 1830. Height: 7½". Courtesy of The Brooklyn Museum.*

CHAPTER IV

The Rococo Revival Style
in American Porcelain: 1840-1850

Between roughly 1820 and 1860, design was dependent upon earlier styles for its inspiration and was characterized by a series of stylistic revivals which adapted the decorative schemes of the past. Generally, the vocabulary of ornament was used faithfully, with simple changes to make it suitable to 19th-century conception. Forms were more freely varied to suit the needs of the moment. Nineteenth-century eyes seemed to require a more realistic approach to detail than those of the 13th through 18th centuries. Therefore, almost unconsciously, the designer tended to transform subtle details in floral ornament to a more realistic context. Furthermore, the 19th century was a period in which many new forms were introduced into daily life. There was more furniture in the 19th-century home and many more objects were used to carry on the ordinary activities of the day. These offered new opportunities for ornamentation.

The use of the earlier styles involved a certain amount of symbolic interpretation. The movement to the Rococo has been explained as a reaction against the Napoleonic era and all that it meant. This cultural return to the style of Louis XV was paralleled by a political return to the old monarchy as Louis Philippe assumed the French throne. The Gothic revival was stimulated in England by the designs and writings of Pugin, who was also a well-known theorist.

In America, one form of the popularization of the ideas of the meaning of style was expressed in A. J. Downing's *The Architecture of Country Houses* (New York, 1842 and later), when he discussed "relative beauty in architecture." He argued that "Gothic architecture . . . should be the style used for all ecclesiastical . . . purposes," and that "in Roman art, we see [the beauty] of the state." In the American interpretation of the 19th-century style, there was a consistently free and fresh approach. Decorative details of an earlier style were used on forms obviously inspired by the early models but adapted to the needs and tastes of the moment. The new approach in pottery was first seen in work done at the Jersey City site of the Jersey Porcelain and Glass Company by its successor, the American Pottery Company.

Although the American Pottery Company made fine earthenwares rather than porcelain, its work reflected the more advanced fashions of the period. A tea set offered in both dark brown and a cream-colored glaze was of Rococo inspiration and consisted of a group of pieces in squat shapes which were covered by floral vines in relief. A spittoon or cuspidor in molded yellow ware depicted eight of the apostles in Gothic niches around the sides. Both examples are in specific styles that were fashionable in the period.

American porcelain made only the smallest concessions to the new fashions and tended to be conservative. The Empire style retained its importance until the late 1840's. The Rococo revival appeared in porcelain as a full-blown style in 1847, when the pottery of Christopher W. Fenton began operating independently in Bennington, Vermont (Plate 11, page 31). The new ware was called parian, or statuary porcelain, and had first been introduced at the Copeland factory in Staffordshire, England, in 1842. Supposedly, one of the Copeland men, John Harrison, had been brought to Bennington to develop the porcelain from local materials. The ultimate products were white figures and ornamental wares with some colored porcelain used in conjunction with white bisque (a porcelain without glaze).

In true Rococo spirit the forms were inspired by 18th-century examples. Relief ornament reflected an interest in naturalism: wild roses, grapes, lily pads, corn and a waterfall were among the subjects used (Plate 15, page 35 and Plate 13, page 33). Figures included popular themes such as the "Greek Slave" by Hiram Powers and sentimental subjects as, for example, a praying girl or Red Riding Hood (Plate 9, page 30; Plate 12, page 32; and Plate 20, page 39). A dinner ware was produced in a richly glazed body.

At various stages of his career in Bennington, Vermont, Christopher W. Fenton had several partners. In 1849 a new plant was opened in Bennington and the name United States Pottery Company came into use, as can be seen in studying the marks used on the wares. The amazing variety of subjects produced between 1847 and 1858, when the plant closed, gives the connoisseur an opportunity to consider several aspects of the American approach to design (Plate 16, page 36). A good many Bennington pieces are based on English models, but the American versions are always subtly simplified to make them fit within the capabilities and needs of the American craftsman. English vases with applied grapes tend to have more delicately formed detail in higher relief than the Bennington product. The Bennington example omits the color change in two-color porcelains, areas in which a change of color would add more to the difficulty of execution than to the attractiveness of the design (Plate 14, page 34).

Certain designs are distinctly American, such as the corn pitchers which reflected the widespread recognition of corn as an American symbol. There is a directness and simplicity in approach that combines with the subject to give the piece an effect that may be considered peculiarly American. Leaving aside the few folk examples made in the Pennsylvania German area a few decades before, the figures made by the Bennington pottery were a new phenomenon on the American scene. Although the sources are most frequently English, the Bennington products were wholly American in spirit and execution.

Around this time, Charles Cartlidge, a Staffordshire native who had been the American agent for Ridgway pottery, established a plant for manufacturing soft-paste porcelain doorknobs and buttons. He went on to produce dinner wares, candlesticks, pitchers, portrait busts and plaques (Plate 19, page 38). His brother-in-law, Josiah Jones, who had experience as a modeler in the Staffordshire region and achieved a fine reputation on the American scene, is thought to have been responsible for making molds for much of the work. Elijah Tatler is credited with most of the painted decoration.

Cartlidge continued his operation until 1856, winning a prize for the high quality of his ware at the Crystal Palace in New York in 1853. The Cartlidge group of bisque busts, plaques and the like probably were made in limited quantity, since the surviving examples have come down in the families of Cartlidge and his partner, Herbert Q. Ferguson. A sculptured hand, in bisque, of Cartlidge's daughter has the delicacy and realism typical of the finest porcelain of the time (Plate 21, page 40).

The pitcher was one of the most popular ceramic forms during the middle of the 19th century. There is a theory that the social custom of the time encouraged the extensive use of pitchers. During the period many silver tankards were remodeled into pitchers. Some historians have attributed this to the fact that the early 19th century was a period of abstinence from alcohol among the upper classes. In both earthenware and porcelain, pitchers were produced in a great variety of designs.

Cartlidge made a number of designs in different sizes with the shapes of the pieces generally curving and squat in a variation of Rococo models in the 18th century. The oak leaf was a popular motif, possibly due to the fame of the Connecticut Charter Oak that was destroyed in about 1850 (Plate 17, page 37). Patriotic symbols such as the flag in a shield and the eagle were also used, and the corn motif that found favor at Bennington appears in a different version at the Greenpoint factory in New York (Plate 22, page 41). This corn mold was taken to the South by Josiah Jones after the closing of the Cartlidge factory.

A neighboring rival company of Charles Cartlidge, William Boch & Brother, also exhibited at the Crystal Palace in New York in 1853, but it has left much less evidence of activity. Boch & Brother had several factories in addition to the one in Greenpoint, and the company used the names Empire and Union Porcelain as well. One marked example of their work is a porcelain pitcher with relief decoration in the form of a cupid

PLATE 9. *Parian figure, "Praying Samuel." Smear glaze on statuette, pillow unglazed. Made by the United States Pottery Company, Bennington, Vermont, circa 1847-1858. Height: 4¾". Courtesy of The Bennington Museum.*

in a bacchic scene, repeating a French 18th-century motif (Plate 30, page 51). Still another pitcher, this one by the American Porcelain Manufacturing Company of Gloucester, New Jersey (Plate 18, page 38), had chinoiserie decoration that was also inspired by the French Rococo. (Chinoiserie were designs in the Chinese spirit, either copies of Chinese models or Western versions of Chinese scenes with figures in Chinese clothing.)

A number of the factories that attempted to produce porcelain before the domestic upheaval of the Civil War are not cited here, since their wares were little different from those of the companies mentioned. The difficulties encountered by these factories were financial rather than artistic. It was close to impossible to compete with the Staffordshire potters, but the Americans, in the field of design, mastered an approach which was characteristically national in spirit.

PLATE 10. *Pitcher with floral motif in full relief. Mark: On the bottom on white paper "Thomas Hart Brewer wrote 'This jug was made by William Laughlin about the year 1852 on Perry Street...this was the first white ware made in Trenton...'" Height: 7". Courtesy of the New Jersey State Museum.*

PLATE 11. *Parian figure, "The Tight Shoe." Made by C. W. Fenton, Bennington, Vermont, circa 1847-1858. Height: 4¾". Courtesy of The Metropolitan Museum of Art.*

PLATE 12. *Parian copy of Hiram Powers' "Greek Slave." Made by the Trenton Pottery Company, Trenton, New Jersey, circa 1869. Height: 12⅛". Courtesy of the Newark Museum.*

PLATE 13. *Pitcher, Niagara Falls design. Made by the United States Pottery Company, Bennington, Vermont, circa 1853-1858. Mark: Scroll shield enclosed "United States Pottery Co. Bennington, Vt." Height: 8¼". Courtesy of The Metropolitan Museum of Art.*

PLATE 14. *Three blue and white porcelain pitchers. Made by the United States Pottery Company, Bennington, Vermont, in the mid 19th century. Mark: On base "USP." Courtesy of The Metropolitan Museum of Art.*

PLATE 15. *Parian pitcher, corn husk design. Made at Bennington, Vermont, circa 1850. Height: 9⅝". Courtesy of The Brooklyn Museum.*

PLATE 16. *Pair of parian figures, "Boy and Girl Reading a Book." Made by the United States Pottery Company, Bennington, Vermont, circa 184*
1858. Height: 10". Courtesy of The Bennington Museum.

PLATE 17. *Pitcher, oak leaf design. Made by Charles Cartlidge & Company, Greenpoint, New York, circa 1850. Height: 13". Courtesy of The Brooklyn Museum.*

PLATE 19. *Candlestick. Attributed to Charles Cartlidge &*
Company, Greenpoint, New York, in the mid 19th century
Height: 9¼". Courtesy of The Brooklyn Museum.

PLATE 18. *Pitcher with mask under spout. Made by the American Porcelain Manufacturing Company, Gloucester, New Jersey, circa 1854-1857. Mark: Initials impressed in paste "APM Co." Height: 8¼". Courtesy of The Brooklyn Museum.*

PLATE 20. *Parian figure, "Autumn," with elaborate applied decorations. Made by the United States Pottery Company, Bennington, Vermont, 1847-1858. Height: 10". Courtesy of The Bennington Museum.*

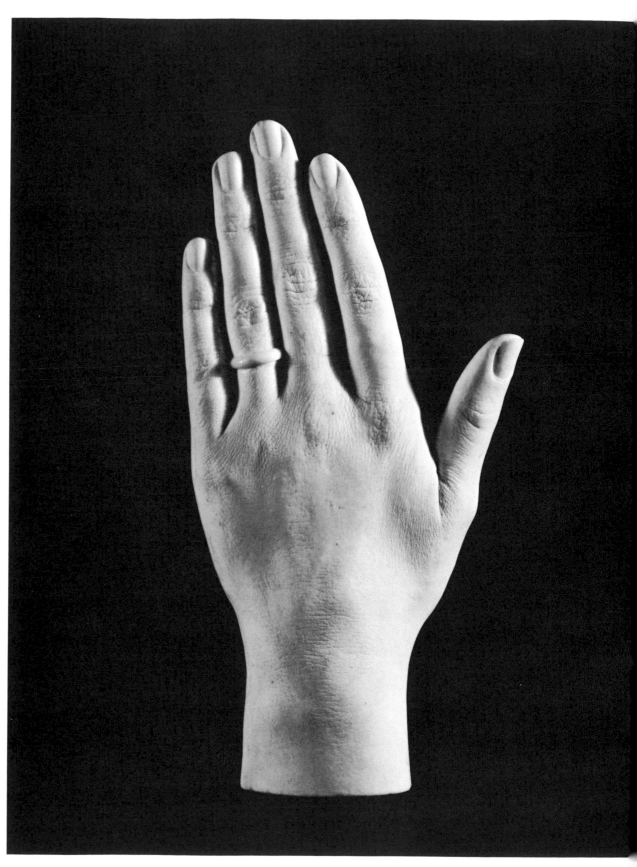

PLATE 21. *Bisque cast of the left hand of Ann Cartlidge Tyndale. Made by Charles Cartlidge & Company, Green-point, New York, circa 1849-1856. Length: 7¼". Courtesy of The Brooklyn Museum.*

PLATE 22. *Pitcher with corn design in relief designed by Josiah Jones. Made by Charles Cartlidge & Company, Greenpoint, New York, circa 1850. Height: 6". Courtesy of The Brooklyn Museum.*

CHAPTER V

Eclecticism in American Porcelain: 1860-1890

Shortly after the Civil War, a radical change occurred in the approach to design. The new approach, given the name "eclecticism," was clearly a reaction to the earlier concepts of design, which were determined by an awareness of the historical context of the arts. Eclecticism was a gathering of various styles to create a new one. Those impatient with the purer revivals of the earlier 19th century now borrowed freely and somewhat indecisively from other periods.

It had been the vogue in the 1840's and the 1850's to use a single style in a specific circumstance, such as the furnishing of a room. After the middle of the century, designers were more concerned with finding appropriate ornament that would be correct for the working of a form without keeping to a style. Decorative details rather than styles were selected from the earlier vocabularies of ornament and the criterion for determining what was suitable depended upon the appearance of the decoration when applied to a workable form.

The most serious exponent of the new approach was the English essayist, William Morris, whose concern for improving design resulted in the formation of the most influential decorating firm of the period. Morris attracted artists to the field of designing for the decorative arts. He inspired a revival of the crafts tradition, and strived to make the public aware of the elements of good design. On a less intellectual and more popular level, there were similar reactions to historicism. And the efforts of Morris and his followers found many imitators.

The eclectic tendency in late-19th-century design may be traced in two directions. On the one hand there were the completely original designs which, aside from those in the *art nouveau* style, were a medley or pastiche of traditional motifs. Exotic Near-Eastern and Oriental shapes and decorative schemes were juxtaposed with those in the Western tradition, achieving entirely new effects. In seeking new approaches and new sources of design there was a great deal of energy spent on exploration. New areas of inspiration were deemed as important as new combinations of ornament.

In porcelain, the exotic played an important role since there was a mystique about the Oriental origins of the material. New forms based on Near-Eastern and the rare Oriental models were exploited, but there was also interest in devising new forms in the Western tradition. This meant creating free, functional variations of forms that had been introduced to porcelain by goldsmiths in the 18th century.

Very significant for the medium was the development of techniques for making refined bodies through technical improvements. After the centuries-old search for the secret of porcelain making, many prized formulae were suddenly made obsolete by a series of discoveries that affected the whole technology of ceramics. Thinner and harder bodies were perfected for the finest wares, and these advances were as much a part of the American scene as the European.

The 1870's were a period of rapid growth for the industry throughout the Western world. The old problems of finding clay and scratching for bare subsistence were forgotten as the industry expanded. Making porcelain became one aspect of a larger field. Equipment for chemistry, sanitary wares and the like were being made as well as decorative objects. Since the designs of this period are challenging and puzzling to the taste of many connoisseurs today, closer attention should be paid to the qualities of production in the era after the Civil War. The industry was highly concentrated in centers that produced every type of pottery ware.

In 1876, an article on the ceramics exhibition of the Centennial Exposition held in Philadelphia reported: ". . . the chief centers of production are Trenton in New Jersey and East Liverpool in Ohio." Typical of the period is the criticism made of the exhibition by another writer: "Whatever the cause there was a thorough lack of artistic pottery of American make at the Philadelphia Exhibition." This went a bit too far. Objectively comparing the American products with those of other exhibitors, their level was high although the examples were less elaborate.

One of the most interesting factories of the period was the Union Porcelain Works of Greenpoint. In about 1861, the company was acquired by an architect, Thomas Smith, and thereafter it developed along artistic lines. By the time of the Philadelphia Exposition the company could show a rather impressive group of pieces that had been designed by the sculptor, Karl Müller (Plates 24 and 25, page 46). A good example of Müller's designs, though it is hard to take seriously today, was a tea set with human heads as finials (a Negro head on the sugar cover and a Chinese head for the teapot cover), a goat as the handle of the creamer and rabbits as legs for all the pieces in shapes which echo Rococo ornamentation to a great degree (Plate 27, page 48 and Plate 28, page 49). Popular symbolism as expressed by Müller was obvious, and every viewer could understand what was represented in his designs.

The Union Porcelain Works also was responsible for a handsomely conceived group of bisque figures, although to some viewing the work in the 20th century, the sentimental tendency they represent so well has limited appeal. The Blacksmith and the portrait bust of Mr. Smith's grandson are well executed in the realistic idiom of their time (Plate 33, page 54 and Plate 34, page 55).

James Carr, of the New York City Pottery, was one of the pioneers in Rockingham-type brown-glazed earthenware. The New York City Pottery went on to produce significant porcelains including a series of parian busts in the 1870's (Plate 37, page 58 and Plate 38, page 59).

An article in *Harper's Magazine* in 1881 described Trenton as the "Staffordshire of America." The high quality of the artistic work done there was cited as proof, and the author put particular emphasis on work that can be attributed to Professor Isaac Broome, a sculptor, who was in the employ of Ott & Brewer. The article noted his "bust of Cleopatra in parian and the pair of vases [which] illustrate the national sport of baseball." These were in the popular version of the eclectic style (Plate 35, page 56; Plate 40, page 61 and Plate 41, page 62). Ott & Brewer also produced fine portrait busts in parian and elaborate decorative pieces in a finely-glazed body which reflected the period's interest in freely combined ornamental expressions. After 1882, belleek, an egg-shell porcelain, was introduced from Ireland and used extensively. This was an unusually thin body, perfect for small display pieces (Plate 43, page 64 and Plate 44, page 65).

Ott & Brewer were one of several companies to make the thin ware. The Greenwood Pottery Company (founded in 1861 as Stephens, Tams & Company) produced stone china up to 1876, then produced translucent china for hotel use. Still later, the company made a ware that was similar to the thinnest porcelain of the Royal Worcester Company of England. This so-called Worcester body was also produced by the Willets Manufacturing Company in a number of elaborate Near-Eastern shapes with heavy gilt decoration.

Beginning in the last decade of the 19th century the Ceramic Art Company, later known as Lenox, developed a particularly fine belleek body used for vases, bonbon dishes and other fancy ware (Plate 51, page 71; Plate 53, page 72 and Plate 54, page 73).

In 1839, East Liverpool, Ohio, became the site of a pottery when the Bennett family established themselves there. By the 1850's, its strategic location had attracted a number of other potters and East Liverpool had achieved a prominence in ceramics. It is best known for making a special version of belleek, called lotus ware. This was perfected at the factory of Knowles, Taylor & Knowles, who also made hotel wares. The light body was used for thin-shell forms, vases and ewers that reflected the Near-Eastern vogue (Plate 48,

PLATE 23. *Bisque plaque. Made by Hugh G. Robertson, Chelsea, Massachusetts, circa 1878-1880. Diameter: 8". Courtesy of The Brooklyn Museum.*

page 69; Plate 50, page 70; and Plate 55, page 74). By the time of the Columbian Exposition in 1893 in Chicago the Knowles Company had a pâte-sur-pâte (paste on paste, imitation of cameo) to exhibit which was very similar to one made at Minton's in England under the direction of M. Marc Solon, a French potter who went to England and became one of the great figures in porcelain making in the late 19th century. Classical forms and elongated versions of Classical figures were used for this cameo-like medium which consciously revived one aspect of Roman art.

The eclectic tendency in 19th-century American porcelain had diverse manifestations. The most successful pieces were those made at Trenton and East Liverpool, but to understand the history of porcelain design in America it is necessary to refer to the output of the art potteries which used earthenware and not porcelain. These thrived after the Philadelphia Centennial. Foremost among them was the Rookwood Pottery of Cincinnati, Ohio, founded by Mrs. Maria Longworth Nichols in 1880. The popularity of earthenware was an outgrowth of ladies' interest in china painting, which was given a serious turn under the influence of English potters who were striving for good new designs as they followed the ideas advanced by William Morris.

Having a certain amount of freedom from the pressures of making immediate sales, the Rookwood potters were able to experiment in design and to use the history of ceramics as a book of inspiration. They exploited the many tendencies of their period to create some of the best eclectic designs. Japanese and Near-Eastern models were used along with various Western examples to create a body of work that was an inspiration to all potters in the years before 1900.

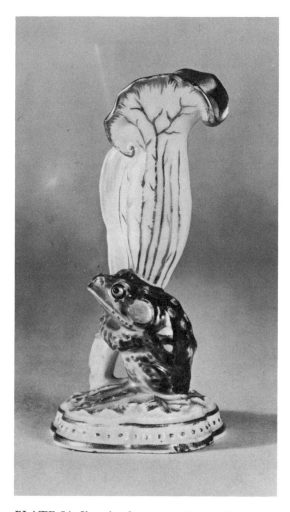

PLATE 24. *Vase in shape of a plant with frog at base. Made by the Union Porcelain Works, Greenpoint, New York, circa 1884. Mark: "U.P.W." with "S" below in gold. Height: 5¾". Courtesy of The Brooklyn Museum.*

PLATE 25. *Vase in shape of plant with turtle at base designed by Karl Müller. Made by the Union Porcelain Works, Greenpoint, New York, circa 1884. Mark: "U.P.W." with "S" below in gold. Height: 5¾". Courtesy of The Brooklyn Museum.*

PLATE 26. *Parian bust of Pallas Athena, Greek Goddess of Wisdom. Made by the Union Porcelain Works, Greenpoint, New York, in the late 19th century. Height: 10". Courtesy of The Brooklyn Museum.*

PLATE 27. *Tea set designed by Karl Müller. Made by the Union Porcelain Works, Greenpoint, New York, circa 1876. Height: tea pot, 6¾"; sugar bowl, 4"; cream pitcher, 3⅞"; two cups, 2⅜". Diameter: two saucers, 5". Courtesy of The Brooklyn Museum.*

PLATE 28. *Bisque "poets" pitcher designed by Karl Müller. Made by the Union Porcelain Works, Greenpoint, New York, 1877. Mark: "U.P.W." on medallion. Height: 7½". Courtesy of The Brooklyn Museum.*

PLATE 29. *Vase, square-shaped body with grotesque lizards on opposite corners. Made by the Union Porcelain Works, Greenpoint, New York, 1884. Mark: Eagle head with "S" in black and impressed on base "U.P.W./1884." Height: 15". Courtesy of The Brooklyn Museum.*

PLATE 30. *Pitcher with molded decoration ornamented with blue and gold. Made by the Union Porcelain Works, Greenpoint, New York, circa 1860. This same mold was used by William Boch & Brother. Mark: Stamped on bottom in black "Manufactured & Decorated/by the/Union Porcelain Co./82 John St N.Y." Height: 8¹³⁄₁₆". Courtesy of The Henry Ford Museum, Dearborn, Michigan.*

PLATE 31. *Bowl. Made by The Wheeling Pottery Company, Wheeling, West Virginia, circa 1904. Mark: "The/Wheeling/Pottery/Co." Height: 2⅞". Courtesy of The Brooklyn Museum.*

PLATE 32. *Vase. Made by the Union Porcelain Works, Greenpoint, New York, 1876. Mark: "Century Vase/Exhibited at Centennial/Exhibition at Philadelphia/Manufactured 1876/by Union Porcelain Works/Greenpoint." Height: 22¼". Courtesy of The Brooklyn Museum.*

PLATE 33. *Bisque figure of a blacksmith. Made by the Union Porcelain Works, Greenpoint, New York, circa 1876. Height: 12¼". Courtesy of The Brooklyn Museum.*

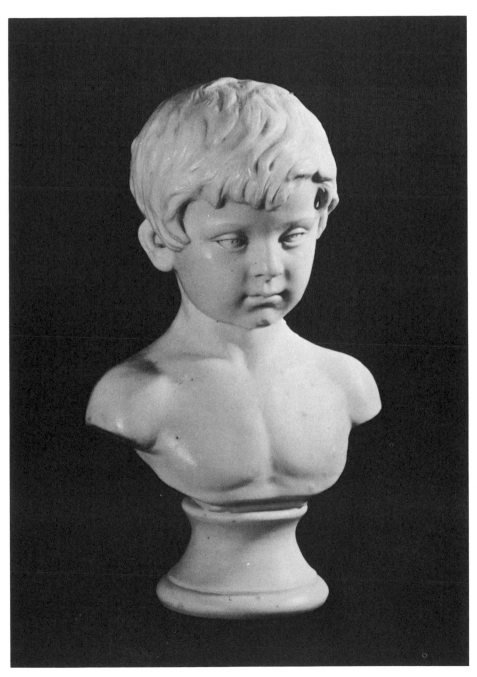

PLATE 34. *Parian bust of Pierre Arsdale Smith, grandson of Thomas Smith, modeled by Karl Müller. Made by the Union Porcelain Works, Greenpoint, New York, in the late 19th century. Mark: "K. Müller." Height: 8". Courtesy of The Brooklyn Museum.*

PLATE 35. *Parian bust of Cleopatra decorated in black, gold and blue and modeled by Isaac Broome. Manufactured by Ott & Brewer, Trenton, New Jersey, circa 1875. Height: 20". Courtesy of the New Jersey State Museum.*

PLATE 36. *Water cooler. Made by the Union Porcelain Works, Greenpoint, New York, 1888. Mark: On base with red transfer "Union/Porcelain/Works/N.Y." and in green transfer print, an eagle's head with an "S" below "U.P.W." Height: 13⅝" Courtesy of The Henry Ford Museum, Dearborn, Michigan.*

PLATE 37. *Parian bust of George Washington. Made by the New York City Pottery, 1876. Mark: Impressed on rear of bust "Manufactured/by/Jas. Carr, N.Y. City Pottery/1876/W. H. Edge/Sculpture." Height: 20½". Courtesy of The Henry Ford Museum, Dearborn, Michigan.*

PLATE 38. *Parian bust of James Carr, modeled by W. H. Edge, one of the principal modelers of the New York City Pottery, circa 1876. Height: 21½". Width: 15". Courtesy of the Newark Museum.*

PLATE 39. *Parian bust of Shakespeare, gray body. Made by Ott & Brewer, Trenton, New Jersey, 1858. Height: 7½". Courtesy of the New Jersey State Museum.*

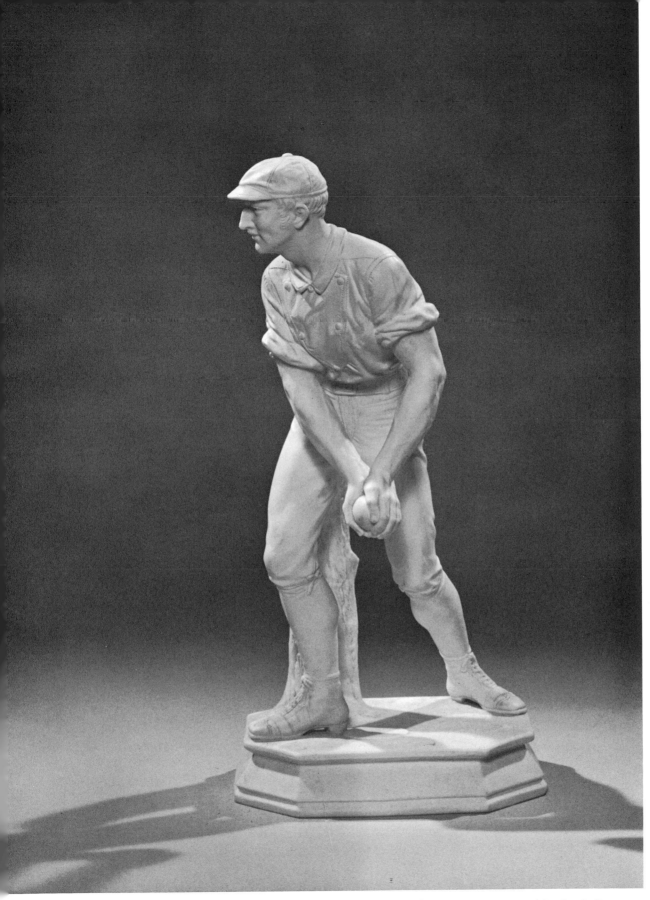

PLATE 40. *Parian figure of a baseball player, "Pitcher," modeled by Isaac Broome. Manufactured by Ott & Brewer, Trenton, New Jersey, 1876. Height: 15". Courtesy of the New Jersey State Museum.*

PLATE 41. *Parian "Baseball Vase" modeled by Isaac Broome. Manufactured by Ott & Brewer, Trenton, New Jersey, 1876. Made for the Centennial Exhibition, Philadelphia. Height: 35". Courtesy of the New Jersey State Museum.*

PLATE 42. *Parian bust of Lincoln modeled by Broome. Manufactured by Ott & Brewer, Trenton, New Jersey, circa 1860. Height: 11½". Courtesy of the New Jersey State Museum.*

PLATE 43. *Belleek sugar bowl, water lily design. Made by Ott & Brewer, Trenton, New Jersey, circa 1876. Height: 5".* *Diameter: 5". Courtesy of the New Jersey State Museum.*

PLATE 44. *Belleek pitcher, bowl, fluted cup and saucer, thistle design. Made by Ott & Brewer, Trenton, New Jersey, circa 1890. Height: pitcher, 6¾"; bowl, 3½"; cup, 2¼". Diameter: bowl, 8½"; cup, 3¼"; saucer, 5½". Courtesy of the New Jersey State Museum.*

PLATE 45. *Gray bisque tea set, George and Martha Washington motif, designed by Isaac Broome. Manufactured by Ott & Brewer, Trenton, New Jersey for the Centennial Exhibition in Philadelphia in 1876. Height: tea pot, 5"; sugar bowl, 2¾"; creamer, 2¾"; three cups, 2¼"; bowl waste 2⅝". Diameter: tea pot, 12"; sugar bowl, 7"; creamer, 7"; three cups, 3⅞"; three saucers, 5"; bowl waste, 8". Courtesy of the New Jersey State Museum.*

PLATE 46. *Parian bust of John A. Roebling. This is one of the last pieces modeled by Isaac Broome. Made by Lenox Pottery, Trenton, New Jersey, circa 1909. Height: 14". Courtesy of the Maddock Collection, Trenton Junior College, Trenton, New Jersey.*

PLATE 47. *Gray belleek woven basket decorated with a rim of modeled flowers in color by William Bromley, Sr. Manufactured by Ott & Brewer, Trenton, New Jersey, circa 1890. Length: 8½". Width: 6½". Depth: 3½". Courtesy of the New Jersey State Museum.*

PLATE 48. *Belleek bonbon dish designed by Joshua Poole. Manufactured by Knowles, Taylor & Knowles Company, East Liverpool, Ohio, circa 1888-1898. Mark: "KT&K Co Lotus Ware." Diameter: 4¾". Courtesy of The Brooklyn Museum.*

PLATE 49. *Belleek picture frame with lilies-of-the-valley in high relief surrounding an oval frame, modeled by William Bromley, Sr. Manufactured by Ott & Brewer (Etruria Pottery), Trenton, New Jersey, circa 1882-1892. Width: 8⅞" x 11". Courtesy of the New Jersey State Museum.*

PLATE 50. *Lotus ware rose bowl. Made by Knowles, Taylor & Knowles Company, East Liverpool, Ohio, 1897. Height: 8". Courtesy of The Henry Ford Museum, Dearborn, Michigan.*

PLATE 51. *Belleek swan bonbon dish. Made by the Ceramic Art Company, Trenton, New Jersey, circa 1889-1894. Mark: "C.A.C." and "Belleek." Height: 4¾". Courtesy of The Brooklyn Museum.*

PLATE 52. *Belleek ram's horn vase. Made by Ott & Brewer, Trenton, New Jersey, 1890. Height: 4". Length: 6". Courtesy of the New Jersey State Museum.*

PLATE 53. *Parian vase carved by Miss Kate B. Sears. Manufactured by the Ceramic Art Company, Trenton, New Jersey, circa 1889-1904. Mark: Inscribed in script on the bottom "Ceramic Art Co. / K. B. Sears / November 21, 1891." Height: 9¾". Courtesy of The Henry Ford Museum, Dearborn, Michigan.*

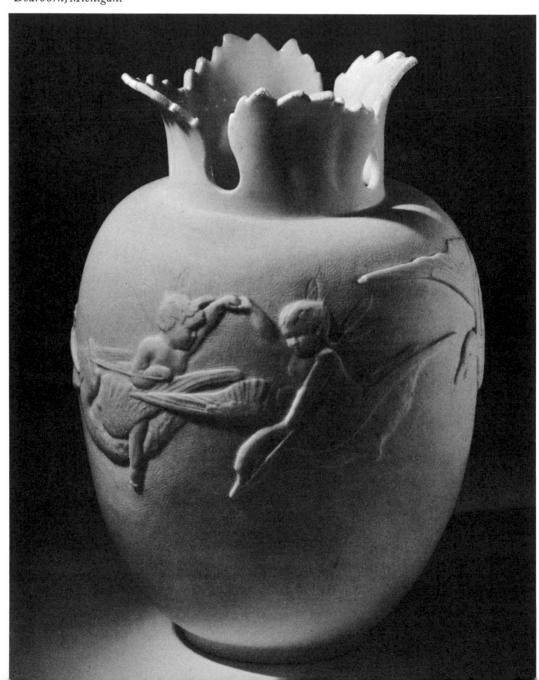

PLATE 54. *Belleek shell vase. Made by Walter Scott Lenox, circa 1887. The porcelain body is thin and translucent. Courtesy of the Newark Museum.*

PLATE 55. *Lotus ware vase. Made by Knowles, Taylor & Knowles, East Liverpool, Ohio, circa 1890. Mark: "Lotus Ware" and decorator's initials "RMB." Height: 10⅛". Courtesy of The Henry Ford Museum, Dearborn, Michigan.*

PLATE 56. *Lotus ware pitcher with floral and leaf design around neck with base surrounded by banding of gadroons and dots, designed by Kenneth P. Beattie. Manufactured by Knowles, Taylor & Knowles Company, East Liverpool, Ohio, circa 1888-1898. Height: 6". Courtesy of The Brooklyn Museum.*

PLATE 57. *Belleek vase with flowers and bird decoration. Made by Ott & Brewer, Trenton, New Jersey, circa 1883-1892. Mark: Crescent with initials at each end and "Trenton" in center, "N.J." below the crescent and "Belleek" above. Height: 10¼". Courtesy of The Brooklyn Museum.*

CHAPTER VI

Porcelain in the 20th Century: 1900-Present

Twentieth-century design is difficult to characterize because we are too close to the subject to define objectively the main currents of style. The different approaches to design today all seem to fit within a range established by the major tendencies of 19th-century design: historicism and eclecticism.

Historicism, or the revival and refinement of a specific earlier style, began in the 19th century, and remains essentially the inspiration for traditional design in the 20th century. It involves the use of historic styles in free adaptations to meet the requirements of the new period. In modern times another facet of historicism is the careful reproduction of objects, reflecting a widespread interest in antique collecting.

Eclecticism has affected 20th-century design in several ways. On a superficial level, decorative details of the past are used to embellish forms of the present, much as they were used in the 1880's. More fundamentally, the philosophy of William Morris, which was expressed first in eclectic design, led to advances and variations such as the *arts and crafts movement,* involving a highly selective continuation of eclecticism, and the *art nouveau,* which was less successful in its attempt at creating a new ornament than in being a delightful expression of the *fin de siècle* mood. Ultimately, Morris' suggestions and his questions on quality in designs were made a part of 20th-century thinking by their influence on one of the prime organizations that helped to form the basic principles of design in the 20th century, the Bauhaus.

The Bauhaus school attracted painters, sculptors and architects who worked together on a re-evaluation of design. This represented the first attempt to reconcile art and the machine, and it made "Bauhaus" the term applied to most modern design in Germany in the 1920's. Within "Bauhaus" there was an effort to consider all problems of design from a fresh and intentionally naive point of view. The artist would question the function of the object, and speculate on the ideal shape for its most efficient employment. He would seek out the best materials to make the needed form, without referring to earlier examples that might cause tradition to affect his design.

The approach of the Bauhaus designer was influential, and much of the functional design that was executed from the 1920's to the 1960's stems directly from the thinking of the school. This has resulted in an avoidance of ornamentation based on traditional decorations, as well as the development of a new idiom in which the natural textures of materials are exploited for their decorative qualities.

Parallel with the Bauhaus approach was that of the designers who worked out a translation of the traditional idiom of decoration to a more contemporary one by simplifying forms in the manner of the Synthetic Cubists, such as Léger. They were responsible for the squat forms with curving ends, and for the generally slick surfaces favored in the 1930's. This decorative tendency was later responsible for the long, sinuous forms that echoed *art nouveau* in the 1950's and 1960's.

In porcelain, 20th-century currents have run strongly in conservative directions, possibly because porcelain is a material that represents stability and quietly announces affluence in the home. From the beginning of the century, reproductions of 18th-century designs have been popular, and actual repetitions of the early models have been supplemented by new work designed in the spirit of the 18th century.

Through the early years of this century, most American factories produced wares that were technically among the best made, although their output could not be considered adventuresome because of their emphasis on manufacturing for a mass market. Their timidity in design was typical of all efforts that flow from a desire to please mass taste. Americans seemed inclined to avoid difficulty by doing what had proven successful when done by others.

Since the late 1930's, however, there has been a sharp reduction in the number of factories and a notable shift in attitude, which marks a very significant turn in the history of American porcelain design. Modern designs were first attempted in the years before World War II. The more experimental American work was made in heavier bodies than porcelain, and was in the crafts tradition of the artist-craftsman operating on a small scale. He did not need to sell a quantity of his work and therefore did not have the same limitations as the porcelain designer whose work had to be in the idiom that would have mass appeal. These artists and craftsmen exploited the beauty of the material with great skill, and their designs had sufficient appeal to sustain and encourage continued experiments.

Generally speaking, porcelain figures in the 20th century have followed the innovations of sculptors; and from the beginning of the century there has been a tendency toward simplifying detail. This tendency was first seen in the work of the Copenhagen factories, and became the established approach in many areas, including the United States. To appeal to a wide audience, subjects usually were kept amusing and handsome. The intimate scale of the medium inspired figures and groups that were pleasant, sometimes sentimental, but always warm and uncomplicated. Representations of people proved perennially popular, perhaps because they were almost always kept simple; and such subjects

PLATE 58. *Meadowlark. Made by Edward Marshall Boehm. Height: 8". Collection of the New Jersey State Museum.*

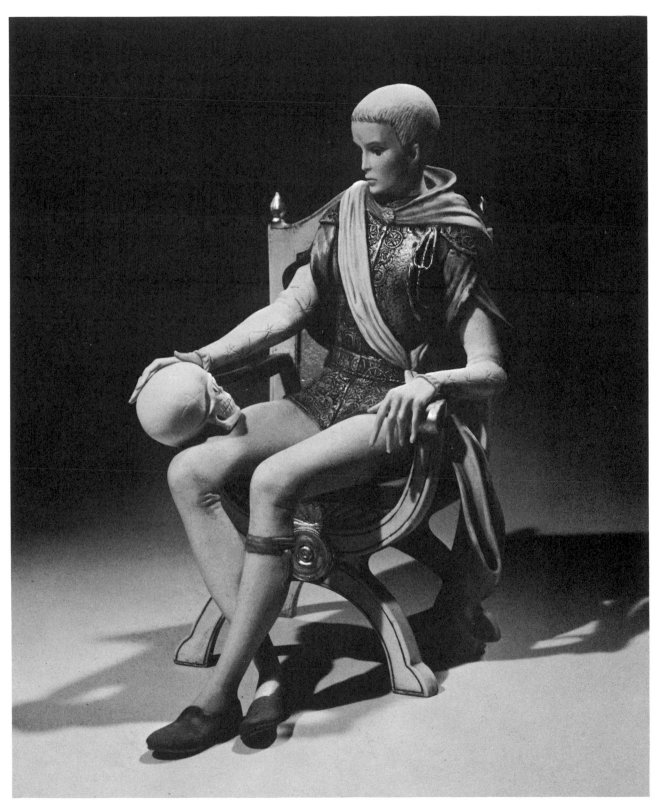

PLATE 59. *Hamlet. Made by Cybis Porcelains, Trenton, New Jersey. Height: 12". Collection of the American Shakespeare Festival Theatre and Academy, Stratford-on-Avon, Connecticut.*

as birds, small animals and flowers interested a few skilled artists and a numerous public.

However, in recent years artists and craftsmen have turned away from simple designs. There has been a resurgence of painstaking craftsmanship which aspires to an ever higher degree of detail. These craftsmen have found abundant inspiration in the world of nature. Birds, flowers and animals have been closely studied and faithfully rendered. A prime example of this approach is seen in the work of Edward Marshall Boehm. The Meadowlark (Plate 58, page 78), reflects Boehm's articulate interest in ornithology and shows how well a bird can be represented in bisque. Mr. Boehm's training in animal husbandry played a vital role in his skillful handling of such difficult subject matter. In the early 1950's, Boehm became a manufacturer, producing small ceramic figures, animals, bowls and vases under the name Osso Ceramics. Osso has since evolved into Edward Marshall Boehm, Inc., which skillfully combines artistic achievement with popular taste and broad distribution. Boehm now specializes in the manufacture of a series of bird scenes.

Cybis Porcelains, in Trenton, New Jersey, is a studio dedicated to the design of a broad range of porcelain sculptures. Cybis artists include in their wide-ranging subject matter the world of nature and idealized figures drawn from literature and the theatre.

The porcelain body makes possible an intricacy of design unobtainable in any other medium. In a sense, the naturalistic figures of Cybis are the equivalent in small sculpture of the school of painting represented by Andrew Wyeth, in which the possibilities for fresh observation of the familiar are exploited to the fullest. The literary subjects have the ethereal quality of Raphael Soyer and Isabelle Bishop.

The firm was founded by Boleslaw Cybis, an artist who had pursued a very successful career in Europe during the 1920's and 30's. Among his many honors were the first prize at the Bienale in Venice and the grand prize at the International Exhibition, "Art and Technology" in Paris in 1937. At the invitation of his government he came to America the following year to paint two al fresco murals for the Polish Pavilion in the 1939-40 World's Fair in New York. His work completed, he and his wife Marja, a sculptress, were homeward bound in September 1939 when the Nazis invaded Poland, launching World War II. Mr. and Mrs. Cybis returned to America and became American citizens.

Cybis established a studio, first in New York and two years later in Trenton, New Jersey. The latter move reflected a decisive turn in Cybis' own artistic development, away from painting and, through a series of experimental stages, to porcelain, a medium with which he had been well acquainted in Europe. Trenton was the traditional seat of porcelain making in America, and there he found the facilities, materials and skills necessary to create his works. Cybis quickly won recognition in the medium of porcelain and the limited output of his studio was soon in rising demand. This success did not affect the group of artists gathered around him; the atmosphere remained casual and free. This same spirit still prevails in the cheerful light-filled rooms of the Cybis studio. Each porcelain piece is individually crafted by highly skilled artists and no two pieces are alike.

Cybis Porcelains are known throughout the world. They have been acquired by art galleries in America and Europe. The President of the United States deems Cybis porcelains suitable for gifts of state (Plates 63 and 64, pages 85 and 86). To mark Pope Paul's historic visit to America, Cybis created a magnificent enthroned figure of St. Peter (Plate 69), which was presented to the Pontiff by Francis Cardinal Spellman during the Pope's peace mission to the United Nations. Even more elaborate is the Cybis sculpture, "The Holy Child of Prague" (Plate 71), first made for the National Shrine of the Immaculate Conception in Washington, D.C. A work of amazing delicacy and intricacy, "The Child" is depicted in his rich traditional garments of silk, brocade and lace. The transparency of silk was achieved by shaving the porcelain to rose-petal thinness, and the brilliant brocade of the cape was created by repeated firings of 24-carat gold.

Because so few pieces have survived, American art porcelain has long been neglected by historians. But this old medium is undergoing a process of renewal. The transactions in porcelain of the leading art auction houses in London and New York bear witness to the fact that men are placing ever higher values on the intangibles of craftsmanship and creativity. Growing popularity and rising artistic standards provide reason to believe that the brightest chapters in the history of American porcelain lie ahead.

PLATE 60. *Ballerina, "On Cue." Made by Cybis Porcelains, Trenton, New Jersey. Height: 12½". Collection of Princess Christina, Stockholm, Sweden.*

PLATE 61. *Beatrice. Made by Cybis Porcelains, Trenton, New Jersey. In commemoration of the 700th anniversary of Dante's birth. Height: 12". Collection of the Damon Runyon Fund.*

PLATE 62. *Turtle Doves. Made by Cybis Porcelains, Trenton, New Jersey. Height: 12". Collection of the American Embassy in Rome.*

PLATE 63. *Bull. Made by Cybis Porcelains, Trenton, New Jersey. Height: 15". Width: 12". Collection of the President of Mexico, Gustavo Diaz Ordaz.*

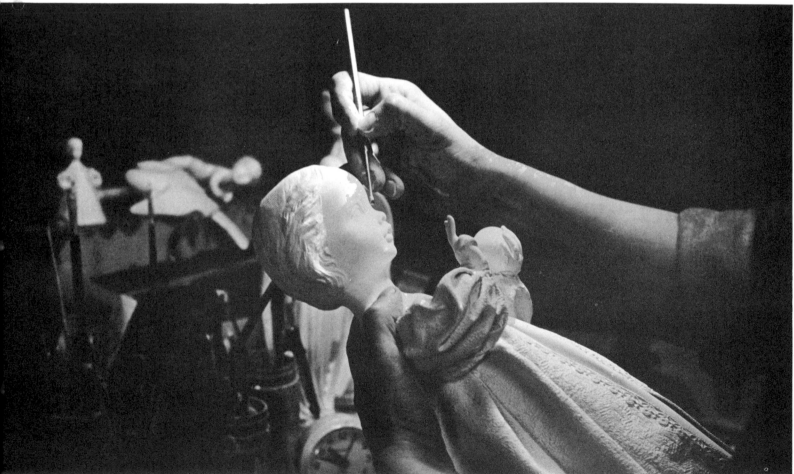

PLATE 65. *Little Blue Heron. Made by Cybis Porcelains, Trenton, New Jersey. Height: 9½". Collection of the New Jersey State Museum.*

PLATE 66. *Flower Bouquet of the United States. Each state flower is represented in this work, which was originally presented at the 1964-1965 New York World's Fair. Made by Cybis Porcelains, Trenton, New Jersey. Collection of the Smithsonian Institute.*

PLATE 67. *Great White Heron. Made by Cybis Porcelains, Trenton, New Jersey. Height: 19". Collection of the American Consulate, Montreal, Canada.*

PLATE 68. *Iris. Made by Cybis Porcelains, Trenton, New Jersey. Height: 16½". Collection of His Royal Highness, Prince Philip, The Duke of Edinburgh, Buckingham Palace.*

Heads of Boy and Girl. Made by Cybis Porcelains, Trenton, New Jersey.

PLATE 69. *St. Peter. Made by Cybis Porcelains, Trenton, New Jersey. Height: 24". Collection of The Vatican, Rome.*

PLATE 71. *Holy Child of Prague. Made by Cybis Porcelains, Trenton, New Jersey. Height: 22". Collection of the National Shrine of the Immaculate Conception, Washington, D.C.*

PLATE 70. *Dahlia. Made by Cybis Porcelains, Trenton, New Jersey. Height: 12". Collection of The Brooklyn Museum.*

PLATE 72. *Moses, "The Great Law Giver." Made by Cybis Porcelains, Trenton, New Jersey. Height: 20". Collection of The Vatican, Rome, Italy.*

PLATE 73. *The Christmas Rose. Made by Cybis Porcelains, Trenton, New Jersey. Height: 7½". Collection of The Bennington Museum.*

PLATE 74. *Madonna With Bird. Made by Cybis Porcelains, Trenton, New Jersey. Height: 14". Collection of Governor and Mrs. Richard J. Hughes.*

PLATE 75. *Juliet. Made by Cybis Porcelains, Trenton, New Jersey, for the 400th Anniversary commemorating William Shakespeare. Height: 12". Collection of the Polish National Museum, Krakow, Poland.*

A Bibliography for Further Study

Although American porcelain has not been treated as a separate subject, a number of books give some insight into the early efforts to establish porcelain manufacturing in the United States. The list below emphasizes the 19th century efforts, since more recent production has been all but ignored in serious study. For the 20th century, useful information is available only in periodicals.

Bennington Pottery and Porcelain, Richard Carter Barret (New York, 1958). A comprehensive study of the subject for collectors.

Early American Pottery and Porcelain, John Spargo (New York, 1926). A good account by a fine collector and student.

Notes on American Ceramics: 1607-1943, Arthur W. Clement (New York, 1944). A fine study based on the extensive Brooklyn collection in which the author had been instrumental in forming.

Our Pioneer Potters, Arthur R. Clement (New York, 1947). An unusual account of American pottery and porcelain which glean from relevant inspected documents.

Pottery of the United States, Helen E. Stiles (New York, 1941). One of the few accounts that includes the 20th century.

The Book of Pottery and Porcelain, Warren Cox (New York, 1944). A general survey of the entire field of ceramics which includes good coverage of 20th century work. Mr. Cox knew the contemporary field from personal experience.

The Ceramic Art, Jennie Young (New York, 1879). An early study that gives a good account of the post-Civil War potteries on the American scene by a contemporary observer.

The Pottery and Porcelain of New Jersey: 1688-1900, Newark Museum (Newark, 1947). A catalog of a significant exhibition.

The Pottery and Porcelain of the United States, Edwin Atlee Barber (New York, 1901). The most comprehensive book on the subject.

Tucker China: 1825-1838, Philadelphia Museum (Philadelphia, 1957). The catalog of a comprehensive Tucker exhibition.

Information on the industry that includes accounts of relevant artistic experiments in the late 19th and early 20th century is to be found in several periodicals.

American Potters Journal, published between 1888-1905.

American Pottery and Glassware Reporter, published between 1905-1910.

Pottery and Glassware Reporter, published between 1879-1893.

Interesting accounts also may be found in reports on such exhibitions as the World's Fairs held every few years in Europe and the United States, i.e., Century of Progress Exposition, Chicago, 1933-34.